ALPHABETS

AR

Saw

Satellite

Saxophone

Written by: Narinderpal Singh Dhillon

DhillonVision
Singapore

Dedicated to my two nieces, Kirpa and Asees.

The ones who have brought colour into my life in the same way I hope this book can bring learning and fun to every child who uses this book.

I would also like to thank my family, whose unwavering support was instrumental in the publishing of this book and app.

Technology is invented to make our lives easier. Let's make learning easier.

1

Open mobile app store and download 'Alphabets: AR' app.

5

Video: Press play to learn how to write the letter. Press pause to stop.

2

Open app and point camera to your Alphabets: AR Book.

6

Pictures: View pictures you put in the folder in AR. Tap to go to next picture.

3

Alphabets: Swipe right or left to spin the alphabets.

7

Tracing: Trace alphabets by tapping in Level 1 and swiping in Level 2.

4

3D Models: Tap screen to go through the models beginning with that letter.

8

Music: Tap the highlighted note consecutively to learn new songs.

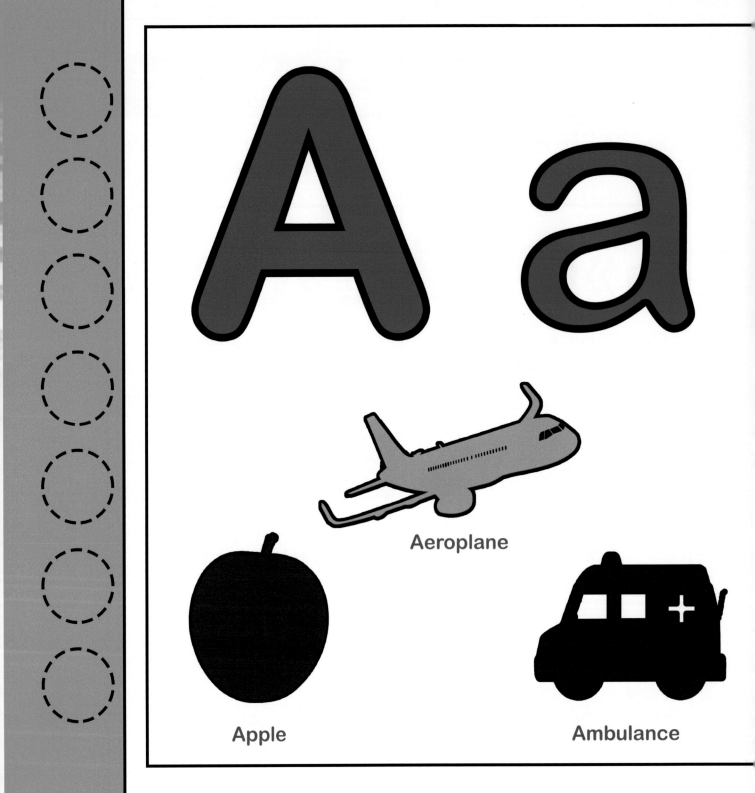

A a

Aeroplane

Apple

Ambulance

B b

Bus

Banana

Ball

Cap

Cat

Cup

D d

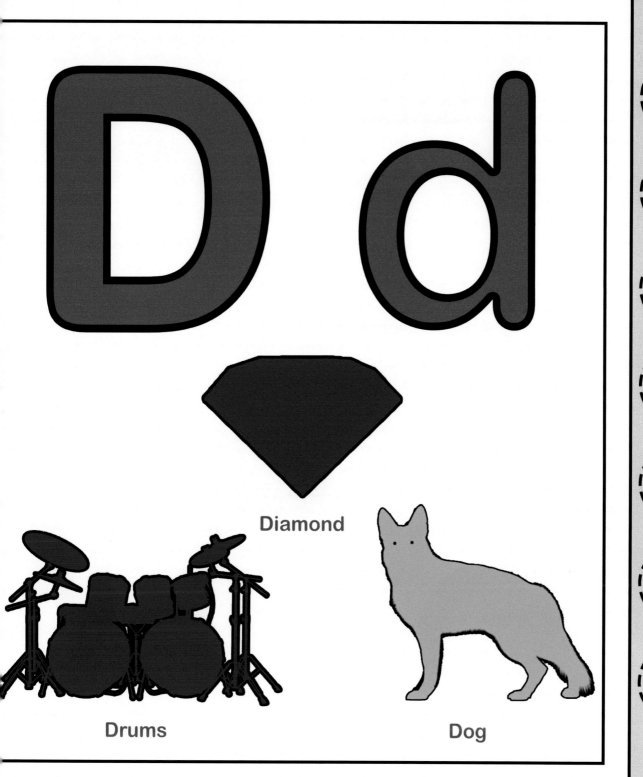

Diamond

Drums

Dog

Eagle

Earth

Eiffel Tower

F f

Fire Truck

Fire Hydrant

Flag

G g

Gate

Gloves

Goat

H h

Hammer

House

Horse

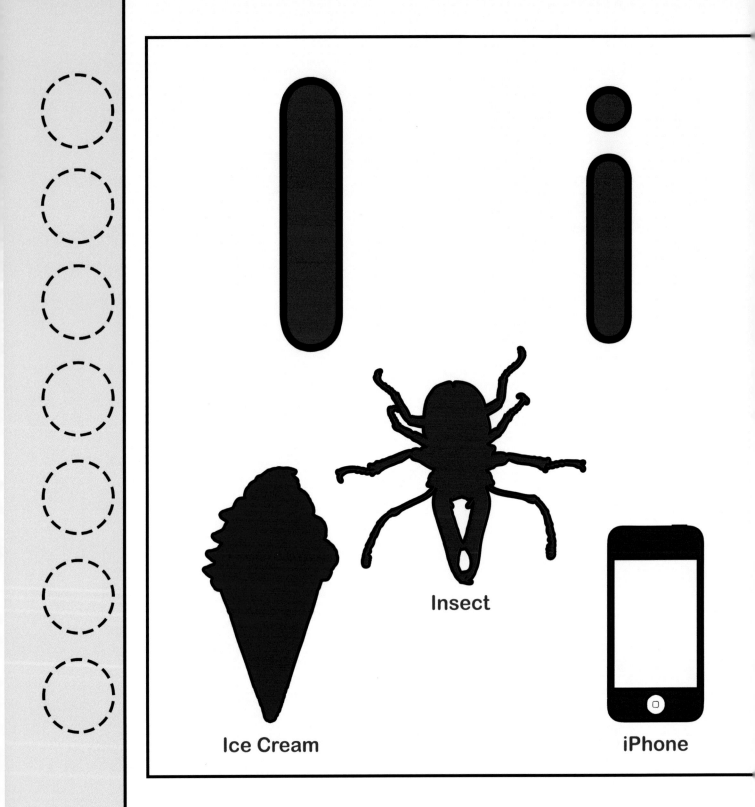

Insect

Ice Cream

iPhone

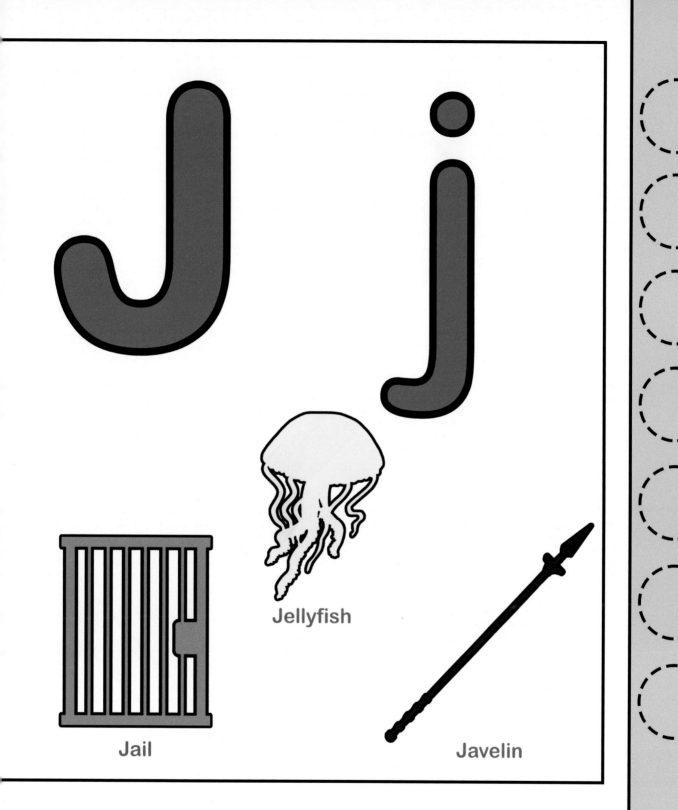

J j

Jellyfish

Jail

Javelin

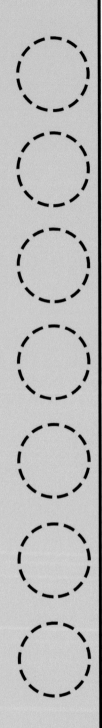

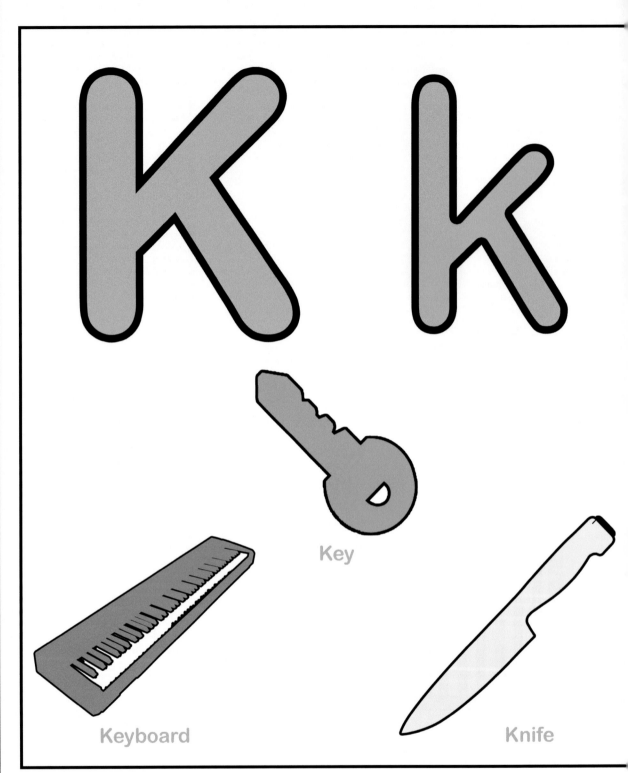

K k

Key

Keyboard

Knife

Love

Laptop

Ladybug

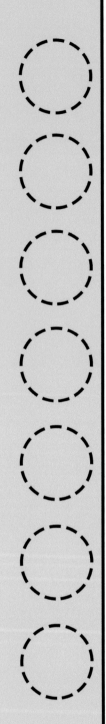

Moon

Microscope

Magnet

Nail

Nine

Note

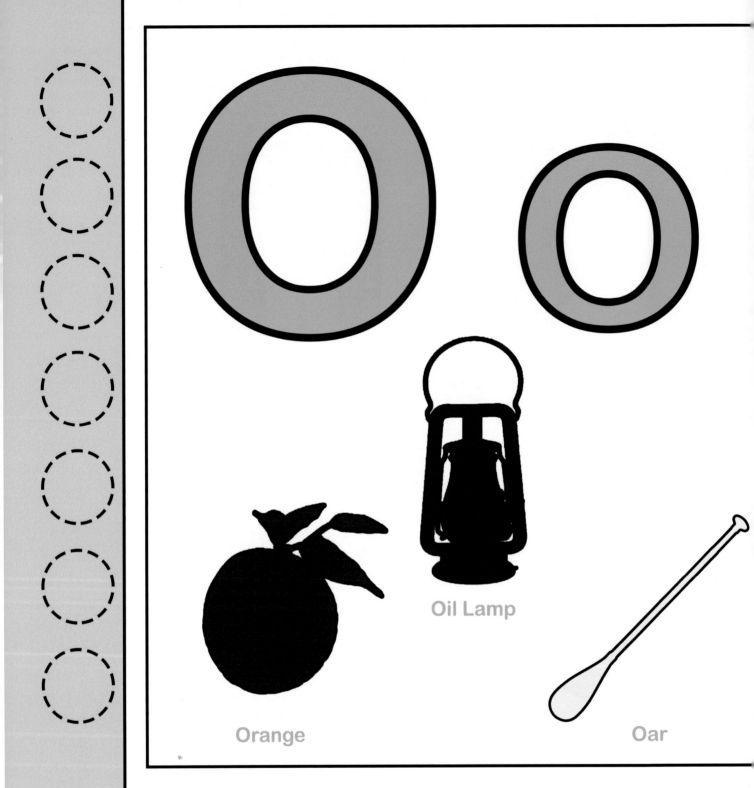

Orange

Oil Lamp

Oar

P p

Pencils

Palette

Pants

Q q

25¢

Quarter

? Question

Quiver

R r

Rhinoceros

Racket

Rabbit

S s

Saw

Saxophone

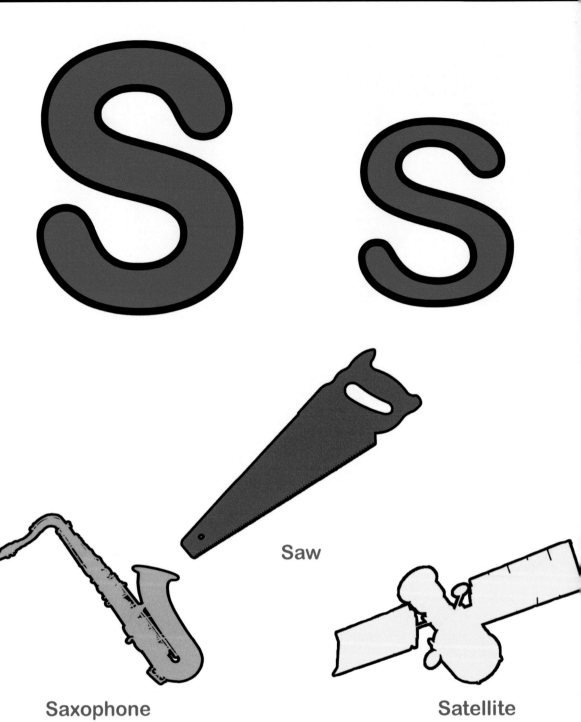

Satellite

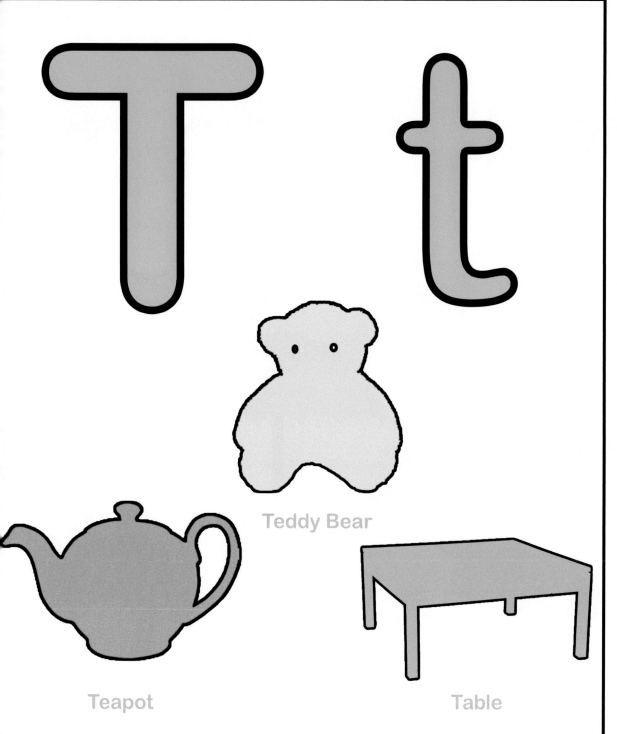

T t

Teddy Bear

Teapot

Table

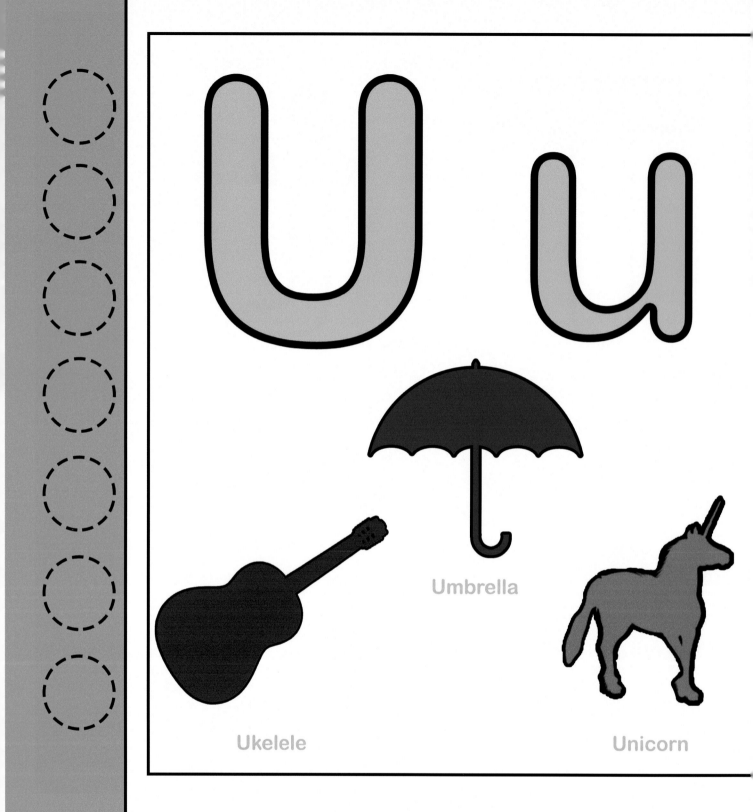

U u

Umbrella

Ukelele

Unicorn

Van

Vase

Vest

Wheelchair

Wolf

Watch

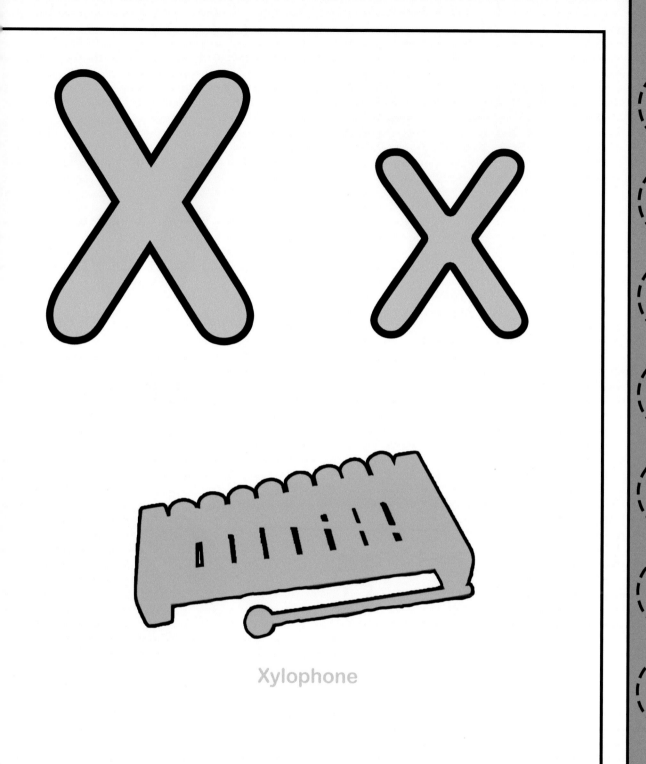

Xylophone

Yacht

Yo-yo

Z z

Zebra

Zero

ISBN
978-1-5437-4819-2 (sc)
978-1-5437-4820-8 (e)

Print information available on the last page.

To order additional copies of this book, contact
Toll Free 800 101 2657 (Singapore)
Toll Free 1 800 81 7340 (Malaysia)
www.partridgepublishing.com/singapore
orders.singapore@partridgepublishing.com

10/02/2018

PARTRIDGE

Printed in the United States
By Bookmasters

04172064-00974430